Restercise

I0154885

3 easy habits to unplug and disconnect

Josiah Pritchard

Published by JPJT Services, LLC

ISBN: 978-1-7365971-1-8

About the Author

Josiah Pritchard has been fortunate to have a front-row seat in the healthcare industry for almost 40 years, including more than 25 years at Mayo Clinic.

As an industry leader, he has worked with America's largest healthcare systems, insurance companies, and employers to design medical and wellness programs. He continues this work as a health and wellness coach, educating and uniting people in protecting, improving, and enjoying their health.

Josiah spent the last several years studying ancient practices, clinical studies, and cutting-edge research - all to answer one question - How can our bodies get more rest? The result of that exploration is the 3 habits in this guide.

Today we know that rest supports our health and our performance. It's not an off switch. You can't catch up later. With these habits, you can return to being still. The habits also improve your mood, help ease any aches and pains, reduce inflammation, rebuild your brain, and refill your spirit.

This program blends modern science with ancient wisdom to uniquely address the physical components of stress-related health problems while simultaneously addressing the emotional.

When not working or typing on his laptop, you can find Josiah enjoying the ocean and walking his bulldogs, Roxie and Darla, in Jacksonville Beach, Florida.

- ✓ 30+ years of working with America's leading employers, insurers, and medical providers
- ✓ 15+ years designing and implementing employee medical and wellness programs
- ✓ 5 + years certified Wellcoach
- ✓ 50+ conferences and educational sessions on health, wellness, and wellbeing

Table of Contents

About the Author ii

Introduction 1

PART ONE: Why Unplug and Disconnect? 9

    4 Myths That Are Holding You Back.............................. 10

    The Unintended Consequences 12

    The Benefits You Are Missing 14

PART TWO: The 3 Habits 16

HABIT 1: Reset Your Level Of Muscle Tension................. 23

HABIT 2: Rebalance Your Nervous System 32

HABIT 3: Refocus Your Attention... 37

PART THREE: The Science.. 46

BOOK BONUS: 10-DAY 3 HABIT JUMPSTART................ 51

Introduction

Do you feel like you are running on empty? Do you worry about your money, your weight, your job, or your relationships? Do you feel physically, emotionally, or mentally exhausted? Do you find it challenging to be still long enough to listen to your body or your spirit?

It's common. Nearly half of Americans (45 percent) lay awake at night in the past month due to stress.

It's because our lives quickly fill with ambitions, deadlines, and competition. We learn we must act, think, eat, move, do more, and continuously improve from an early age.

Before too long, life becomes a never-ending race where the faster you run, the more you sprint to get ahead because there is always someone or something ahead of you. The mantras of modern life are to go faster, do more, and to get the most you can out of life have their place. They serve us well ... up to a point. There comes a time we can't turn it off.

If you're exhausted, drained, tired of it all, outraged, or numb, it's understandable. The problem is when you are stressed, you can't sleep, you can't think, and you can't be your best. The American Psychological Association (APA) annually surveys Americans' relationship with stress — how stressed they feel, what keeps them up at night, and how they deal with the stress in their lives. The APA report, sixty-one percent (61%) of adults say that managing stress is extremely or very important. But only thirty-five percent (35%) say they are doing an excellent or very good job at it. Making it worse, many of the things we turn to can only provide temporary relief when we need lasting change.

Here are four reasons why we need to be still and create calm right now!

1. <u>Rest Is Necessary</u> - Your body will not function at its best when it lacks rest, not just from sleep but from weariness and distress. These habits will let your body remember what it is like to let go of stress and be still.

2. <u>Rest Is Radical -</u> Rest brings our bodies and senses to quiet. In a world that is constantly demanding our attention, we can get used to the noise.

3. <u>Rest Is A Gift</u> - We too quickly tend to push quiet time or self-care aside. We call it "downtime" like it's not essential. Or, we go to another extreme with ideas like "active recovery." But life without stillness is not sustainable. It is part of the natural cycles of our mind, body, and spirit. Being still refreshes our bodies and gives us the energy we need.

4. <u>Rest Is The Foundation for Spiritual Intimacy</u> - In science, it is called energy. In religion, it is called spirit. Among our tribe, we call it vibes. Whichever definition you pick, being still provides the basis for an experience of being one with our chosen faith and beliefs. It creates the space to focus on gratitude, compassion, and forgiveness for yourself and others. It establishes the quiet necessary to hear the still, small voice inside that is your inner compass. When we step back, we create space to protect what matters most: patience, forgiveness, and love.

Clinical studies show information in this guide will help you unlock benefits such as:

- ✓ Improve the quality of your attention
- ✓ Affect your interpersonal behaviors
- ✓ Provide greater empathy and compassion
- ✓ Positive impact on the brain and immune system
- ✓ Assist with chronic pain
- ✓ Help overcome insomnia
- ✓ Slow down forgetfulness
- ✓ Increase the volume in 4 regions of the brain
- ✓ Can help with depression, autism, ADHD

I understand change can be challenging. You are not lazy, unmotivated, or stuck. After years of living in survival mode, you are just tired. That's why the tools I will give you are the easiest, simplest, smallest things you can do to create lasting change. These tools have been proven to work in clinical studies involving thousands of people. Because science shows us it works, you don't need to rely on goals, programs, or motivation. Instead, I will teach you to use your subconscious to create habits, the real key to lasting change. Using evidence based tools also means if you have a nervous system, these habits will work for you. And if you are reading this, I am 100% sure you have a nervous system. Therefore, I am 100% confident these habits will work for you too.

Here's why it matters now more than ever before: today's world is designed to distract you. Our modern world increasingly revolves around the human attention span and how products can capture that attention and take away our focus. This brings unintended consequences for our health. We get thrown out of balance. We forget how to be still. In the modern age, self-care is no longer a luxury. It is self-defense.

We need to step back before we can step up.

I think we have reached a tipping point when we begin to reject the unintended consequences of our modern lifestyles. Increasingly, we see and feel the dangers to our bodies, minds, friends, and communities.

Our healing **begins** on the inside, and that is our responsibility. The people and things around us **maintain** our health. They are also our responsibility.

Fortunately, recent medical and psychological science discoveries have given us new insights into managing stress and creating calm. For example, we used to think of sleep as just the "off" switch, but it is so much more.

We also better understand how the body uses the same pathway, our central nervous system, to help manage our sleep, involuntary systems, emotions, memory, and immune system. We can use these findings from brain science to improve our rest response and support our natural healing processes to create calm.

Are you familiar with the fitness chain Orange Theory? Their founders used exercise science to design an optimal program that increases your metabolism and changes your body from the inside out.

I have used brain science to design an optimal program that decreases your stress levels and changes your body from the inside out. To optimize your inner calm, we can return to some of our most ancient practices, and we can use current medical evidence. For example, new research shows that stress and sleep deprivation result from an autonomic nervous system (ANS) imbalance. Especially in the low activity of the parasympathetic nervous system (PNS). That means when we fix stress, we will also improve our sleep because it's all related. But there is a more significant takeaway we often ignore.

Balance is not something you find.
It's something you create.

Let me illustrate with a quick story about a client Lee. Lee struggled with self-worth and was exhausted trying to please others first. He needed to end his sleep deficit, and he required balance. What Lee needed most was a new perspective. With one of my tools, he created some space to reflect and then refocus - creating time to do things he wanted to do to get back in balance without the guilt.

This is not another book about anxiety... breath deeply, eat right, get enough sleep, meditate, etc...etc....etc...We may cover similar topics, but this guide is easy to read. It clearly explains the most recent science and the newest techniques to unplug, create calm and feel better.

Maybe you have tried…….
- YOGA… but the awkward poses left you defeated.
- JOINING A GYM OR HIRING A TRAINER…but it's confusing, expensive, and hard to be consistent, so you stopped.
- MEDITATION or BREATHWORK…but you couldn't find your Zen, so you gave up.

It doesn't have to be this hard or this complicated. There are little things you can build into your day, throughout the day, every day, to make the load a little bit lighter. This guide will show you how.

People exercise. People meditate. But, for most of us, these are different activities. Science shows we can also combine what works from the two and deliver more results with the least amount of effort, time, training, or costs.

Please do not misunderstand yoga and meditation are excellent activities, and you should enjoy them often. It's just many of us need a step before that so that we can be ready. I've solved that problem for you.

In the same way, you learned to brush your teeth; you can use new habits to improve your relaxation response and your body's natural state of happiness. Each person has this inherent healing capacity. Through small changes in your daily life, you can increase your body's ability to be still.

With repeated practice, your resting heart rate and respiratory rate will decrease. You will operate from a more relaxed baseline while awake. You may experience less pain. You may experience deeply profound moments of inspiration. You will learn tools that you can use yourself anywhere, by yourself or in a group. More experienced users will explore even deeper layers of the mind and awareness.

What's different about this approach

- We use habits, not goals. You have to remember goals. That makes them hard.
- It's fast. It won't take weeks or months to learn or to feel results. It takes only a few minutes each day.
- It's holistic. Compared to other approaches, the 3 habits offer an integrated mind, body, spirit experience. We treat the body, brain, and mind as one.
- There is nothing new to learn. It's already there prewired inside you. We are simply making the body's involuntary responses intended.
- It works. The habits are based on clinical expertise and evidence-based.
- The more you do it, the more automatic it becomes, and the more results you see.

You can use habits to enhance the body's natural relaxation response.

This guide is for people interested in creating a sense of calm and enjoying all the benefits.

This guide is for people who know someone who struggles with stress.

And, this guide is for people who want to start, or restart, your wellness journey. It is also a great compliment to any current exercise or fitness program.

This guide has 3 sections. Part One explains why being still is more important and more challenging to do than ever before. I review the myths that hold you back and the benefits you are missing.

Part Two illustrates the 3 Habits and how to get them started.   Part Three details the science that makes the habits work.   I've got a 10-day 3 habit Jumpstart plan to help you get started in the final section.

PART ONE: Why Unplug and Disconnect?

When is the last time you took a break? Going slower and doing less is not the norm of today's world. We know stress is inevitable and healthy. Only occasionally are we supposed to deal with the threats. But a tragic result of ongoing stress is that people get used to it; it becomes old, familiar, and sometimes almost comfortable, so they ignore it.

Cumulative stress takes place when the inputs in our body like nutrition, sleep, and other forms of recovery cannot fulfill the drainers, like exercise, anxiety, and other things that take away our energy.

If you let the draining tasks in your life accumulate and drain your bucket, once you hit empty, your body will force you to rest through injury and illness.

This happened to my client Kerry. Kerry is a fitness machine. He works out like a professional. One day his back snapped. He went to the doctor and was surprised when the physician said his back was tight as rocks. Kerry needed a recovery plan. He used one of my tools and used rest as a resource to balance the stress, not a way to turn it off.

Kerry is not alone. In a world full of distractions, the times of calm have become too rare. Eighty percent (80%) of all health problems are caused by stress, according to research presented by Dr. Wayne Jonas. He also shows that health does not always come from medicine; most of the time, it comes from peace of mind, peace in the heart, peace in the soul.

Now more than ever, we need a new way to restore our body's natural balance. So why is it we fail so miserably to take the actions we need?   A lot of it has to do with our beliefs.   Our beliefs guide our actions.   Do any of the following assumptions or behaviors resonate with you?

4 Myths That Are Holding You Back

1. *We believe being busy is a badge of honor.* We quickly tend to push rest aside. We call it "downtime" like it's not essential. We pull all-nighters and applaud powering through, like it doesn't have a cost. But life without rest is not sustainable. Rest refreshes our bodies, giving us the energy we need.

   Instead, we try to do everything at once, and we end up wandering aimlessly. You work takes up all your day. Your family and friends take up all your weekend time. The days begin to blur together, and soon you feel exhausted, even when you do sleep.   We know we can't be on 100% of the time, but too often, that is the message we send to our body, and it gets locked in, keeping us out of balance. The reality is we are not busier. Just the opposite is true. The studies show we have not increased the time we spend working in decades. However, recently our time spent sitting has increased by over an hour, from 5.7 to 6.4 hours per day. And, our time on computers outside of school or work has increased twenty percent, to over 2 hours per day.

2. *We believe rest is nonproductive.* It's not. It is one of the most crucial functions for both your physical and mental wellbeing. It helps your body recover and your brain regroup. When we have it, it promotes resilience, growth, flourishing, and joy. It's the secret sauce that allows us to thrive.

3. *We get distracted.* We live in an era of chaos, uncertainty, and constant mass and social media-generated stress. Your diet, your workout, your social media feed, they are all pushing you to go-go-go. But nothing teaches you how to slow down, how to stop, or how to rest. It can create a sense of destination addiction. The idea is that happiness is in the next place, the next job, or the following situation. Until you give up the idea that happiness is someplace else, it will never be where you are.

4. *Many of our activities unintentionally promote our stress response, and very few of our activities add to our rest response.* You have a training plan, a nutrition plan, and a project planner. Professional athletes and elite performers will also have a recovery plan to avoid involuntary injuries and to accomplish more when needed. Do you?

Sometimes we get in the way. Often our suffering doesn't come from what is happening. Instead, it comes from what we are telling ourselves. Our thoughts have tremendous power over how we feel. It's not what you say to everyone else that determines the tone of your life; it's what you whisper to yourself that has the most significant power.

Unfortunately, most of us tend to use harsh, critical language when we talk to ourselves. Consider for a moment, would you talk this way to a close friend or even a stranger? Listen to your inner dialogue. Don't allow yourself to be a bully to yourself.

I hear clients say, "It's too hard. I can't be still. My mind is all over the place. I have too many things to do already." But experience tells me that the more resistant you are, the more you need to try, and the more unexpected benefits you will find.

We need to stop glamorizing overworking. The absence of sleep, good diet, exercise, relaxation, and time with others isn't something to be celebrated. You don't need to burn out or sacrifice anyone, anything, or yourself to reach a goal. When you are rested, really rested from being calm and still, you can learn to adapt your performance to your resources, not a schedule.

The Unintended Consequences

When we worry too much, our nerves become frazzled. Habitual patterns of stress and negative emotions are like junk food - they take away from our health and vitality.

The problem is we can go too hard and not give enough time for rest. Our agendas take over. But productivity and rest and not mutually exclusive. You can go further when you take small breaks to restore your natural balance.

Our ability to regulate our emotions weakens when we are under stress. It makes it hard to stick to a diet or learn new things. When you're stressed, it is easier to continue doing what you have been doing than to change; it is easier to give in to temptation than resist it. It is easier to go on "automatic pilot" than to consider what to do next.

The American Institute of Stress reports the most frequently reported symptoms of stress are sleeplessness, anxiety, body aches, indigestion, and rapid heartbeats.

Stress isn't just in your head. It's a built-in physiologic response. When you are stressed, your body responds. Your blood vessels constrict. Your blood pressure and pulse will rise. You breathe faster—your bloodstream floods with hormones such as cortisol and adrenaline.

When negative thoughts about pain are spinning through the brain like a broken record, it inadvertently activates the brain's danger system. This can send the body into high alert, intensifying pain even further. We begin to accept headaches, feeling negative or overly critical, unexplained exhaustion, irritability. We can experience becoming physically ill, insomnia, endless anxiety, feeling inadequate or hopeless, feeling numb or apathetic about life. We can begin neglecting self-care.

We are beginning to understand better how chronic inflammation can trigger disease processes. We have discovered uncontrolled inflammation plays a part in every disease, including heart disease, diabetes, cancer, and even depression.

Shifts in the inflammatory response from short- to long-lived can significantly alter all tissues and organs. According to research by David Furman published in the Journal Nature Medicine, this can increase the risk for various non-communicable diseases in both young and older individuals.

We can't continue to ignore these warning signs. If you see yourself or someone you care for reflected above, please act. I would share the benefits you will receive if you establish the habits will far exceed any expectations or hesitation you may have now. Very often, a change of self is needed more than a change of scene.

The Benefits You Are Missing

I believe we all can shift our mindset, take worry out of the equation, and make every day a bit better. It is prewired inside us, but too often, our behaviors disrupt our natural signals.

When you are still, you access the body's natural state of happiness. If you spend more time there, you will reap all the benefits. The less time you spend there, you will reap all the consequences.

We can use the science of relaxation response and the science of change to create targeted new default behaviors that complement our natural states. Benefits include stress reduction, improved concentration, a boost in memory, and reduced emotional reactions.

Eighty percent (80%) of your health happens at home, outside of work, outside of the Drs. Office, and the hospitals. With these 3 habits, you can improve three of the four vital signs your doctor uses to measure your health: blood pressure, heart rate, and breathing rate.

We can target the rest response more effectively and efficiently. This allows the body's healing energy, which is usually consumed by our thoughts and our emotions, to be free to operate at its most accelerated and therapeutic level.

Restercise gives you an easy, enjoyable way to survive the stressful demands of modern life and remain healthy - physically and mentally. When you continue to practice the habits, the benefits deepen.

First, you learn to be consistent: a key to lasting change. You recognize your strength comes from what is inside you, not outside. It brings freedom from disturbance and turbulence. Over time you gain the essential capabilities to be agile and resilient.

When you invite stillness, you learn to be an observer. Outside distractions become more diffuse. When the mind is quiet, you can read the compass of your internal feedback, feelings, emotions, and intuition. Without the noise, your inner critic will become your inner champion.

Your readiness is at an optimal level, meaning you have had enough time to recover, and your energy is high, ready for some action.

PART TWO: The 3 Habits

Evidence supports the best way to maintain health is to preserve it through a healthful lifestyle rather than waiting until we are sick to put things right.

It's the things we do most of the time that chart our destination. It is default behaviors, not decisions, that control most of our daily actions. Our subconscious mind runs over 90 percent of our life. That's good news because if your habits got you here, your habits will get you home. We can use them to create calm in the body from the inside out.

When it comes to lasting change, the winning story is evolution, not revolution. Our most repeated physical actions can, with continual practice, be performed automatically without any real-time awareness. By using the central nervous system, you are controlling what is primarily an involuntary system. You are creating a new program in the sensory-motor section of the brain and reestablishing unified communication among bodies' systems. This inner change in brain function makes the possible outer change in muscle function and mood. We think of those skills as being stored in our "muscle memory" but these responses are stored in our brains. Restercise is exercise in rest, and we can use it to learn new responses to relax our whole body.

<u>Let your body remember what it is like to relax, to let go of tension.</u>

Let's start at the very beginning....

I don't want you to start anything new. I would like you to change what you already do, at the time and place most convenient for you.

For example, I'm pretty sure you are doing an adequate job of breathing. You may have been exposed or even tried different types of breathwork. There are lots out there, which is excellent. It gives you a playground to explore.

When we want to be calm, we want the parasympathetic network (PNS) to be dominant. That will trigger other healing systems as well. When the PNS is dominate, we are in balance. We are more open to new people and new experiences. We act with purpose. It is a lot more than "rest and digest". We can use our breath to get us there, and Habit 2 explains how.

So, the question becomes, when. One of the best ways to start a new habit is to anchor it to an existing habit. Likewise, the best way to start is with pockets of time that already exist in your daily routine. You can do each habit in as little as a minute. Here are some examples of when you can practice being still:

- waiting for the coffee/tea to brew,
- before/after a shower or bath,
- sitting in your car waiting for the light to change,
- to transition from work to home or home to work,
- to start your bedtime routine.

With each habit, just start where you are, with one or two minutes a day, and increase the volume over time.

With this technique, you create a ritual. Then, the habit becomes automatic. We can trust the neurons in our brain to do their thing.

This applies to whatever change you have in mind. Transform the big behavior, so it is tiny and specific. Set the bar low. So low you cannot fail.

✓ Reduce stress - Deep breathing for 3 minutes
✓ Strength Train - Do five pushups against the wall
✓ Cardio - Put on your running shoes each morning
✓ Sleep better - Charge phone in a different room
✓ Move more - Stand, don't sit - just for a minute

Make a list of your daily routines. I am sure you will find a few places you can use as an anchor. You won't need it forever. It's like using training wheels when you learn to ride a bike. Very soon, you will have mastered the skill and can do it at will.

Select one habit and focus on one simple thing you can change today. Start with a few small activities that are realistic given your lifestyle, work, and family needs.

Finally, give yourself some grace to find something that works. I give you lots of examples in this guide. Find one you like. You can then build on it until it's more sustainable.

Remember, with these habits you cannot fail. You are giving your body the right conditions to be still, using the language it understands.

To help you along the way. I will have more tips for each habit.   And, at the end of this section, I will give you a 10-Day 3 Habit JumpStart Plan.

Why are there 3 Habits?

Each habit targets a different dimension of your central nervous system. We use the body to control the brain, the breath to control the body, and our thoughts to focus our mind. I cover the science in more detail in Part Three. However, I want to highlight a few key before we begin.

Neurofeedback research shows that we can change the brain by reinforcing specific patterns of connectivity and inhibiting others. We can measure relaxation by shifts in Autonomic Nervous System balance towards increased parasympathetic activity. With these habits, you can consciously control your Autonomic Nervous System and reap the benefits of the Parasympathetic Response.

When the Parasympathetic Network is dominant, the body's functions target healing, regeneration, and nourishing the body. For the mind, psychological qualities include calmness, contentment, and relaxation.

Positive thoughts are more challenging. They take more work. It's why we need to practice. But in a very short time, you can permanently rewire your brain to raise levels of happiness. So, let's get started.

When you learn how to control where your attention goes, you become the master of your mind. When you practice taking mini-breaks, you extend your longevity. You can run further, climb, and accel. But to sustain the pace, you can't let yourself get too empty, by then it is too late. Being still is not just passive rest. Being still leaves you energized and inspired. It allows you to commune in sacred rest and connects to the world inside. It does not mean to be in a place where there is no noise, trouble, or hard work. It means to be in the midst of those things and still be calm in your body, mind, and spirit.

The Nervous System

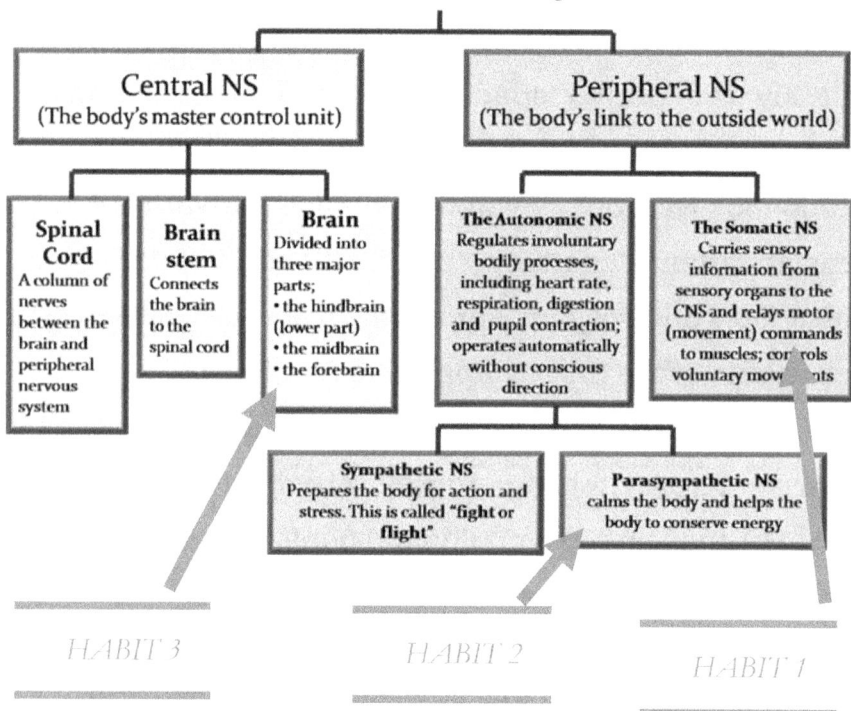

Central NS (The body's master control unit)			Peripheral NS (The body's link to the outside world)	
Spinal Cord A column of nerves between the brain and peripheral nervous system	**Brain stem** Connects the brain to the spinal cord	**Brain** Divided into three major parts; • the hindbrain (lower part) • the midbrain • the forebrain	**The Autonomic NS** Regulates involuntary bodily processes, including heart rate, respiration, digestion and pupil contraction; operates automatically without conscious direction	**The Somatic NS** Carries sensory information from sensory organs to the CNS and relays motor (movement) commands to muscles; controls voluntary movements

Sympathetic NS Prepares the body for action and stress. This is called "fight or flight"	**Parasympathetic NS** calms the body and helps the body to conserve energy

HABIT 3   HABIT 2   HABIT 1

We can use the brain and nervous system to our advantage. At any time, we can use the science of the relaxation response and the science of change to create targeted new default behaviors that complement our natural states.

HABIT 1. Reset your body.

Slow, gentle movement rewires the peripheral nervous system. Keep your body active, but not too much.

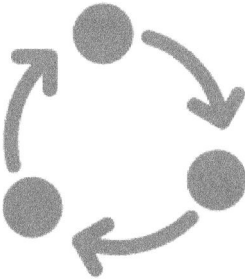

HABIT 2. Rebalance the brain. We can use breath to turn off our arousal systems and turn on the parasympathetic network. When you slow down and focus on the out breath, you calm down the brainstem arousal system.

HABIT 3. Refocus your mind.

You can use your thoughts to rewire the prefrontal cortex and build a happier you.

There are little things you can quickly build into your day, throughout the day, every day, to make the load a little bit lighter:

•   a more gentle way to move to reset the level of tension in our muscles

•   a softer breath to turn off our arousal systems, and

•   a kinder thought to focus on kindness, compassion, and appreciation.

  Next, I review each habit in more detail. In each section, you will get an opportunity to practice and learn how to master each habit.

HABIT 1: Reset Your Level Of Muscle Tension

For most of us, our modern lifestyles are both sedentary and repetitive. We build up muscle tension by sitting down for much of the day, and when we do exercise, we tend to do the same things and not have much variety in our movement.

In this habit, we unwind the tension held in the body. A finger flick and lifting 50 lbs. involves the same number of nerves. We will take advantage of our body's established connections with a bit of twist. Sometimes, an unusual approach can get us to the right destination.

We can do less. Doing less avoids strain and inflammation. We will prevent extensive long stretches. Instead, we will go slower.

In addition, we will focus more on the release because that is not what your brain expects. The result will increase awareness and tell your brain to lower your resting muscle tone.

We do very little, but this stage is firing up all 100 million neurons in your body. It's like pressure washing your autonomic nervous system and clearing out those cobwebs.

Stretching is commonly used as a technique for injury prevention. Stretching is traditionally used as part of a warm-up to increase flexibility or pain-free range of motion (ROM) about a joint to promote better performances and reduce the risk of injury. There are three common types of stretching:

static, ballistic, and Proprioceptive Neuromuscular Facilitation (PNF).

If you usually stretch or use a roller to release your muscles, you may have noticed that the results don't last very long. The level of tension does not live in our muscles; our nervous system controls our muscle tension. Therefore, we need to actively retrain our nervous system to reduce our resting level of muscle tension for more than a few hours.

Research by Tudor Bompa reveals low-intensity stretching is likely to result in small-to-moderate beneficial effects, without creating muscle damage and inflammation markers, compared with high-intensity or no stretching.

The next time you want to stretch, try this:

* Further contract (firmly but gently) the muscle that feels tight. Do this purposefully and keep within your comfort range.

* Then slowly lengthen that contraction, as if you were just waking up in the morning and yawning.

* Then completely relax.

This activity is called Pandiculation. Pandiculation provides feedback to the nervous system. It results in more relaxed muscles while providing greater muscle control and coordination.

Pandiculation occurs in most animal species. A yawn is an example of Pandiculation. When we yawn, the body does an internal system check and reappraisal to help us get ready for whatever may be next.

If you have ever seen a dog or cat arch its back when they get up from a nap or watch a baby stretch their arms and legs as they wake up, you have observed the particular response.

Pandiculation is associated with the arousal system. It's our natural way to reset the central nervous system and respond to a buildup of tension in our muscles. Based on the level of contraction in our muscles, the nervous system restores our sense of balance, our level of muscle tension, and the equilibrium of the myofascial system.

However, we don't need to limit the benefits to isolated moments of involuntary action. We can consciously target the brain in the same manner. In that way, we can get all the benefits, like releasing accumulated tension and the brain opening the gate to relaxation whenever we want.

Here is an example. I call it the Corkscrew. You can use it to check your current level of muscular awareness. I've got a video on YouTube for you as well.

When we sit too much, and our muscles stay contracted. Our brain, which controls the muscles, forgets how to relax our tight muscles resulting in Somatic Muscular Amnesia.

Our brain forgets what we don't use and does less for what we use often. Therefore, retraining the nervous system can release chronic muscle tension and create change in muscle memory.

Corkscrew	Cue
You can do this movement sitting.	Keep your torso, shoulders, and head aligned. Keep your lower body as still as possible as you rotate.
This sequence will re-pattern the major muscles of the back, shoulder, neck, and hips. There are five sets of instructions. You are tightening, then slowly lengthening, the muscles in the direction you turn. Think of turning and twisting your spine the way you uncork a bottle. Then, uncork a bottle to celebrate!	**Target Areas** 1. Relieves chronic pain in muscles of the entire back, shoulders, neck, and hips. 2. Relieves eye strain and relaxes the muscles in the face. 3. Increases flexibility with the core muscles surrounding the spine. 4. Increases range of motion for twisting left and right. 5. Regains strength and efficiency of muscle coordination. 6. Improves posture.

Starting position: Sit tall at the end of the chair. Bring your knees out wider than your hips, keeping your knee perpendicular to your ankles.

Sequence 1: Very slowly turn your whole torso to the right, rotating the eyes, head, shoulder, elbow, and torso as far as is comfortable. If you feel a stretch, pull back. Repeat for a total of 3 times. At the 3rd turn, stop at your point of comfort. Look over your right shoulder. With your eyes open, notice the direction of your nose. Pick a spot on the wall or floor to mark your "before" point. Return to center.

Sequence 2: Place your left hand on your right shoulder, with your elbow relaxed on your chest. With your eyes open, twist slowly to the right. Repeat for a total of 3 times. Contract a little more each time. Think of twisting the screw deeper into the cork. Return to center. Relax completely.

Sequence 3: Turn your head and torso to the right. Holding the torso in this position, turn the head only back to the right. Repeat for a total of 3 times. Return to center. Relax completely.

Sequence 4: Lower your left hand. Let your fingertips touch your chin. Turn your head and torso to the right. As your torso twists right, keep your head centered over your chest. Keep your head, shoulders, and torso moving right. Move only your eyes to gaze to the left. Repeat for a total of 3 times. Return to center. Relax completely.

Sequence 5. Now repeat the pattern we used at the start. With your eyes closed, very slowly turn your whole torso to the right, rotating the eyes, head, shoulder, elbow, and torso as far as is comfortable. If you feel a stretch, pull back. Repeat for a total of 3 times.

At the 3rd turn, stop at your limit. Look over your right shoulder. Check to see if your nose is pointing to a spot further than your original checkpoint. This is your "after." Is it different from where you started? That is not a change in muscle; it is a lasting change in your nervous system.

CONGRATULATIONS! You just activated your brain's motor and sensory command centers. You reawakened mitochondria inside dormant muscles. And you reprogrammed your brain and peripheral nervous system.

You can use this technique with any stretch. Instead of the traditional stretch and hold for 30 seconds, try this:

1. CONTRACT
2. SLOWLY LENGTHEN
3. FULLY RELAX

Always move slowly and try to make it smooth. Never force or struggle. Moving with intent will retrain your nervous system. Explore the different sensations in your body as you change the movements.

Here is one more example you can use to practice. Most everyone has attempted a toe touch exercise. Standing toe touches are about as old-school as an exercise can be, but that doesn't mean they're too old-fashioned to work. They are often considered a measure of hamstring flexibility. However, toe touches are not just about flexibility. They have a lot to do with your overall health. When done properly, standing toe touches work your abdominal muscles. They also stretch and work your calves, your hamstrings, your butt, and your shoulders.

A stretching routine is often promoted as the best way to improve your toe touch abilities. Most stretching exercises will instruct you to hold the stretch at a point of mild discomfort for 30 seconds and then repeat it. Ouch!

Hamstrings that need stretching are, obviously, too short. Why is that? How is that? Simple: those muscles are holding tension -- that is, contracting. Most often, we are keeping tense by habit, unconsciously.

That is why hamstrings (and other muscles) tighten up again so soon after stretching or massage. Better results come by changing the "set-point" -- our sense of what "relaxed" is. Changing the set-point requires more than stretching, manipulation, or massaging; it requires learning new movement/muscle-memory -- and unlearning the old muscle/movement memory.

Don't think about "touching your toes" or getting into extreme positions. Instead, the focus is on drawing the mind inward and becoming aware of the sensation that each exercise produces.

Focus your energy only on the muscles that are being strengthened. We leave the rest of the body as relaxed or uninvolved as possible.

Starting position: Plant both feet on the floor hip-width apart. Make sure that your toes are pointing straight forward with your knees aligned over them. Keep your legs straight, but do not lock them.

Movement: Breath in and then slowly exhale as you slowly bow down to reach your first easy limit. It's OK to let your back round up a little bit because trying to keep it perfectly straight can strain your lower back.
Breath out. Round your back and come up a bit.
Relax and inhale. Come down a bit. Allow you back to arch.
In a series of exhale, curling forward and inhale arching backward, come up a little bit less, and down a little bit further each time. It may be helpful to think of pushing from your hips, instead of bending.
When done, let your arms hang for a moment.
Return to an erect posture.
Allow the body to rest completely.

I have a few more examples for you at the back of the book. They are just a place for you to start. Take your time and do what feels good for your body. Only you know what's right for you.

How to start this habit?

✓ When you catch yourself stretching involuntarily, like a yawn, try this instead.

✓ Try this as an alternative to one of your current stretches.

What's the goal for this habit?

✓ As needed to relax a tight muscle.

✓ Preventive: Try to reset one muscle group per day.

✓ Integrate several movements into a routine.

When do I do this habit?

✓ Start with one movement for one minute and increase as needed.

Where do I do this habit?

✓ You can do these movements anywhere. You can be standing, sitting, kneeling, lying down.

Additional Resources.

Search for Somatic Exercises, Pandiculation, or Thomas Hanna.

Some yoga studios will offer a class. Ask for one!

HABIT 2: Rebalance Your Nervous System

A common characteristic of yoga and meditation (coming up) is using a slow, deliberate breath. Research now shows breathing links to brain function and behavior.

According to researchers at Northwestern University, the typical respiratory rate in humans is within the range of 10 - 20 breaths per minute. Slow breathing is defined as any rate from 4 to 10 breaths per minute. Their studies show using an inhalation of 3 seconds and exhalation of 6 seconds results in the highest activation of the autonomic nervous system tone. This allows the PNS to become predominant, causing the body to relax quickly. In other studies, a shift towards parasympathetic balance in healthy humans was reported in people who breathed at eight breaths per minute instead of 12 and 16 breaths per minute.

Heart Rate Variance (HRV) studies paint a similar picture. The maximum HRV is typically also observed at about a respiratory frequency of 6 breaths per minute.

These studies illustrate that breathing is more than a passive function; it is an active signal to our body. Your breath can be like the oar of a boat and steer you towards still waters and of parasympathetic dominance, promoting recovery and resilience throughout the body.

To get a slower breath of 8 breaths, we need to follow a tempo of 50 beats per minute. You can use an online metronome as a guide to help you get started.

To turn off the arousal system, we want to focus on the exhale. We will also breathe in and out through the mouth. Olfaction, or smell, is the most powerful sense that provides us information about a threat. Your nose is directly connected to your brain and hard-wired to engage your arousal systems. When you breathe through the mouth, you don't encounter that part of your nervous system. Give this a try,

➢ Breath in for a count of 3
➢ Breath out for a count of 6
➢ Breath deep into the belly

How long you want to go is up to you. It is easier to start with shorter sessions:

- 10 Soft Breaths will take 90 seconds
- 20 Soft Breaths will take 3 minutes
- 30 Soft Breaths will take 4 and 1/2 minutes
- 50 Soft Breaths will take 7 and 1/2 minutes
- 100 Soft Breaths will take 15 minutes

How to start this habit?

✓ Start with one session one time a day. It will become automatic very fast.

What's the goal for this habit?

✓ Try for 30, 50, or 100 soft breaths.

When do I do this habit?

✓ As needed to destress and relax.
✓ Preventive: Try to practice at least once per day. Use the same time and place every day if you can.
✓ Integrate before or after other habits.

Where do I do this habit?

✓ Anywhere except underwater. Do not attempt if oxygen is not present.

Additional Resources. Our goal is to create calm, but there are many types of breathwork. Explore online and find what you like. How many different styles can you try in a week? Ask in your local gym or yoga studio. Sometimes they will offer a breathwork class.

Breathing exercises can help with a range of medical conditions, particularly stress and anxiety. They are most effective as part of a daily routine. People can try breathing techniques for the first time when they are calm and breathing normally. They may find it beneficial to practice at the same time every day. Becoming familiar with a breathing exercise can take time. Here are seven ways to breathe.

Pursed lip breathing

▪ breathe in through the nose

- breathe out through the mouth with pursed lips
- make the breath out twice as long as the breath in

Diaphragmatic breathing

- place the hands lightly on the belly
- breathe in through the nose until the belly rises
- breathe out through the mouth for twice as long

Mindful breathing

- find a quiet place without distractions
- choose a comfortable position, ideally sitting or lying down
- focus on breathing by feeling and listening to the body inhale and exhale
- allow thoughts to pass through the mind without judgment

Deep breathing

- sit somewhere comfortable and consciously relax the shoulders
- inhale slowly, filling the lungs
- exhale slowly, emptying the lungs completely
- It may help to count to four for each breath.

Box breathing

- breathe in through the nose for a count of four, filling the lungs
- hold the breath in the lungs for a count of four
- breathe out slowly through the mouth for a count of four, emptying the lungs fully
- wait for a count of four before breathing in again

Alternate nostril breathing

- close the right nostril with the thumb of one hand

- breathe in through the left nostril
- close the left nostril with the fourth finger and release the thumb
- breathe out through the right nostril
- breathe in through the right nostril
- close the right nostril with the thumb and release the fourth finger
- breathe out through the left nostril

4-7-8 breathing

- breathe in through the nose for a count of four
- hold the breath for a count of seven
- part the lips and exhale loudly for a count of eight

HABIT 3: Refocus Your Attention

The average adult brain creates approximately 70,000 thoughts each day. During this time, the brain is designed to seek out a threat, keep you safe from danger and protect you. As a result, your brain focuses on the negative.

It seeks out what's wrong instead of what's right. It holds on to adverse events and feelings more than positive ones. It tells you that if you were just this or just that if you could try a little more complicated, then things would be better. It often creates problems that don't even exist.

How can you counteract this natural tendency toward the negative? We deny it by changing to focus your attention on loving-kindness, compassion, and forgiveness. Giving or receiving compassion can make us healthier and happier. This takes intention and effort, which is why we need to practice.

While we don't fully understand what happens in the brain, evidence indicates that we use different neural pathways when we pay attention to the present moment. It appears focusing our attention activates pathways in the prefrontal and somatosensory cortex to repair and rebuild the wiring that protects the brain against anxiety.

It's common for your mind to wander during meditation, no matter how long you've been practicing. Meditation is not about turning off thoughts or feelings; it's about learning to observe them without judgment. Meditation is about receiving. Noticing and savoring the pleasant moments, even if you fake it, can strengthen positive emotions.

If you're not sure how to practice self-compassion, try a loving-kindness meditation. Here's one you can do alone or with a partner. You can read and record this script to playback. Speak slowly. Your brain will mirror your speech, so use that to slow it down.

Begin with five to 10 minutes of reflection. Start by choosing a verbal affirmation that is meaningful to you. Take a few deep breaths. With full intention, repeat your chosen affirmation.

As you continue to practice, feel free to extend these well-wishes to others. Here are some examples:

May I be happy.

May I be healthy.

May I be kind to myself.

May I experience love and joy.

May I live life to the fullest extent.

May I accept myself, just as I am.

May I feel peace and contentment.

CONGRATULATIONS! You redirected your brain's attention and engaged the prefrontal cortex, shutting down the amygdala. You power washed away the cortisol and inflammation. And you started new neural networks that will help you alleviate stress, recover faster, and improve your mood. Remember, the more you practice, the greater the results.

It may feel awkward or even silly at first but allow yourself to explore this idea. Not only does compassion decrease suffering by helping those in need, but also it can boost your bond with others.

Although the practice of meditation has ties to many different religious teachings, meditation is less about faith and more about altering consciousness, finding awareness, and achieving peace. There isn't a right or wrong way to meditate. It's different for everyone. It's essential to find a practice that meets your needs and complements your personality.

Still not sure meditation is right for you? Here are some other ideas.

Perform a random act of kindness for a friend, colleague, or stranger. Notice a difference in your mood or stress levels afterward. The joy you'll feel after committing a random act of kindness will give you a sense of joy that money just can't buy.

The next time you encounter a difficult person or circumstance, try responding with compassion. Ask yourself, "Why is this person suffering?"

The next time you greet a friend, don't ask, how are you? Or, what's new? Ask, what happened today that was good? Create a conversation that inspires. Dig for gold, not for dirt.

In a study by Dr. Amit Sood, participants who counted their kind actions for a week became happier. Consider counting your previous two kind actions right now after you finish reading this paragraph. Likely, this simple activity will enhance your self-worth.

Further, counting kindness might inspire you to do more acts of kindness so that you could count them later. That's a nice positive feedback loop.

How to start this habit?

It's best to start in small moments, even 5 or 10 minutes, and grow from there. Couple that with an additional 2 to 5 minutes of meditation throughout the day to break up the chaos, and you will soon be feeling the benefits. Here are a couple of ways to get there

- ✓ On the hour for one minute
- ✓ AM and PM for 10 minutes
- ✓ Once a day for 20 minutes

What's the goal for this habit?

- ✓ You should sit in meditation for fifteen to twenty minutes every day.

When do I do this habit?

✓ The Canadian Police meditate before starting the day to improve decision-making and deal with situations more calmly, without agitation.

Where do I do this habit?

✓ You can find it in nature, but you can also nurture it yourself. A calm, quiet space is preferred. Using the same place helps.

✓ Using incense or essential oils can also be helpful. It creates another layer of our senses. Studies have shown positive effects of lavender aroma on sleep.

Additional Resources. Develop a few healthy affirmations that will keep you mentally strong. As you progress, you can listen to your favorite meditation on YouTube or apps like Insight Timer and Headspace. Look for META, Loving Kindness, or Forgiveness. This is not a time to clear your head. We want to fill it.

Ask in your local gym or yoga studio. Sometimes they will offer a meditation class.   Here are seven different styles of meditation to consider.

Mindfulness meditation

In mindfulness meditation, you pay attention to your thoughts as they pass through your mind. You don't judge the thoughts or become involved with them. You simply observe and take note of any patterns.

This practice combines concentration with awareness. You may find it helpful to focus on an object or your breath while observing any bodily sensations, thoughts, or feelings.

This type of meditation is suitable for people who don't have a teacher to guide them. You can easily practice it alone.

Spiritual meditation

Spiritual meditation is used in Eastern religions, such as Hinduism and Daoism, and Christian faith. It's similar to prayer in that you reflect on the silence around you and seek a deeper connection with your God or Universe.

Essential oils are commonly used to heighten the spiritual experience. Popular options include Frankincense, myrrh, sage, cedar, sandalwood, palo, and santo.

You can practice Spiritual meditation at home or in a place of worship. This practice is beneficial for those who thrive in silence and seek spiritual growth.

Focused meditation

Focused meditation involves concentration using any of the five senses. For example, you can focus on something internal, like your breath, or you can bring in external influences to help focus your attention.

Try counting patterns you see, listening to a gong, or staring at a candle flame. This practice may be simple in theory, but it can be difficult for beginners to hold their focus for longer than a few minutes at first.

If your mind does wander, it's important to come back to the practice and refocus.

As the name suggests, this practice is ideal for anyone who requires additional focus in their life.

Movement meditation

Although most people think of yoga when they hear movement meditation, this practice may include walking through the woods, gardening, qigong, and other gentle forms of motion.

It's an active form of meditation where the movement guides you.

Movement meditation is suitable for people who find peace in action and prefer to let their minds wander.

Mantra meditation

Mantra meditation is prominent in many teachings, including Hindu and Buddhist traditions. Mantra meditation uses a repetitive sound to clear the mind. It can be a word, phrase, or sound, such as the famous "Om." It doesn't matter if your mantra is spoken loudly or quietly. After chanting the mantra for some time, you'll be more alert and in tune with your environment. This allows you to experience more profound levels of awareness.

Some find it easier to focus on a word than on their breath. This is also a good practice for people who don't like silence and enjoy repetition.

Progressive relaxation

Also known as body scan meditation, progressive relaxation is a practice to reduce tension in the body and promote relaxation.

Often, this form of meditation involves slowly tightening and relaxing one muscle group at a time throughout the body.

In some cases, it may also encourage you to imagine a gentle wave flowing through your body to help release any tension. This form of meditation is often used to relieve stress and unwind before bedtime.

Visualization meditation

Visualization meditation focuses on enhancing relaxation, peace, and calm by visualizing cheerful scenes or images.

With this practice, it's important to imagine the scene vividly and use all five senses to add as much detail as possible.

Another form of visualization meditation involves imagining yourself succeeding at specific goals intended to increase focus and motivation.

Many people use visualization meditation to boost their mood, reduce stress levels, and promote inner peace.

PART THREE: The Science

Stress is inevitable and healthy. Our body and brain are designed to maintain the status quo, reduce thinking, and preserve balance. Only occasionally are we supposed to deal with the threats.

What causes stress for a person is highly individual. A common example is having to speak in public. Some people find it easy to give a speech in front of a crowd. However, for others, the same situation may feel nothing short of dreadful and causing worry for weeks in advance. A stressful experience can also be quite positive, like getting married or walking into a room where friends and family are hiding on your birthday. Surprise!

We have learned that even low to moderate levels of experienced distress can heighten the risk for a chronic condition later in life. Chronic inflammation can trigger disease processes, and uncontrolled inflammation plays a part in every disease, including heart disease, diabetes, cancer, and even depression.

To help keep the balance, our Nervous System is the highway for every thought, feeling, sensation, and movement—every second, 100 billion neurons process 1 trillion sensations. Studies show our health depends on a well-balanced nervous system, cycling between alertness and rest. Stress and the resulting hormone release, eating habits and digestion, body temperature, and other essential bodily functions can influence the ability to recover and perform at our best.

Twenty-five years of research by HeartMarth, including over 300 peer reviewed studies, reveals that in general, emotional stress - including anger, frustration, and anxiety—gives rise to heart rhythm patterns that appear irregular and erratic. In contrast, positive emotions send a very different signal throughout our body. When we experience uplifting emotions such as appreciation, joy, care, and love, our heart rhythm pattern becomes highly ordered, looking like a smooth, harmonious wave.

We also better understand that every time we have a thought, we make a chemical. These neurohormones focus your attention and motivate you to take action. For example, cortisol is nature's built-in alarm system. It's your body's primary stress hormone. It works with certain parts of your brain to control your mood, motivation, and fear. It motivates you to protect yourself.

Other thoughts create different chemicals. Dopamine is responsible for sending the message, "I've gotta have it; go get it. Once you get whatever you've "gotta have" or need, the chemical Serotonin is released. Serotonin sends the message, "ahhhh, mission accomplished." When serotonin levels are normal, one feels happier, calmer, less anxious, more focused, and emotionally stable. It's one reason we like to check our email, social feeds, and text messages.

When we generate positive thoughts, when we feel happy or optimistic, cortisol decreases. Interestingly, ninety percent (90%) of our serotonin receptors are in our gut. And your adrenal glands -- triangle-shaped organs at the top of your kidneys -- make your cortisol. It really is all connected.

The term "Relaxation Response" was introduced in 1975 by Dr. Herbert Benson, professor, author, cardiologist, and founder of Harvard's Mind/Body Medical Institute. The response is defined as your personal ability to encourage your body to release chemicals and brain signals that make your muscles and organs slow down and increase blood flow to the brain.

The Relaxation Response is essentially the opposite reaction to the "fight or flight" response. According to Dr. Benson, using the Relaxation Response is beneficial as it counteracts the physiological effects of stress and the fight or flight response.

According to Dr. Benson, one of the most valuable things we can do in life is to learn deep relaxation — spending some time quieting our minds to create inner peace and better health.

The National Center for Complementary and Integrative Health (NCCIH), part of the National Institutes of Health (NIH), reports that relaxation techniques help manage various stress-related health conditions. This includes anxiety associated with ongoing health problems and in those who are having medical procedures.

Evidence suggests that relaxation techniques benefit symptoms of post-traumatic stress disorder (PTSD) and may help reduce occupational stress in health care workers.

A range of research has examined the relationship between exercise and depression. This includes evidence that yoga, as adjunctive therapy, may be helpful for people with anxiety symptoms.

Stress management programs commonly include relaxation response techniques. These include breathing techniques, muscle relaxation, guided imagery (focusing the mind on positive images), autogenic training, biofeedback, and self-hypnosis.

The goal is similar in all: to consciously produce the body's natural relaxation response, characterized by slower breathing, lower blood pressure, and a feeling of calm and wellbeing. The 3 habits have the same goals.

Being Still corrects an imbalanced nervous system.

The more time you spend under stress, the less you can rest. Your body is in one state or the other. It cannot be in both at the same time. We can measure the ANS/PNS balance using Heart Rate Variance. Many activity trackers and body sensors monitor Heart Rate Variance (HRV). And more traditional measures, like heart and respiratory rate, can also provide a way to measure stress in the body.

Looking at your nightly HRV averages can help you prioritize rest (lower than average) or know if you are ready for a challenge (higher than average).

BOOK BONUS: 10-DAY 3 HABIT JUMPSTART

When to comes to health changes, most people start strong and do OK for three to four weeks, but then they slowly revert to old habits. Instead, we will begin with a few small things. Remember to give yourself some grace to find something that works. You can then build on it until it's more sustainable.

You cannot fail. You are giving your body the right conditions to be still, using the language it understands. Keep what you like. If you don't like it, try something else. Just be consistent.

By the end of 10 days, you will have learned and practiced the 3 habits. You will gain the knowledge and ability to create calm and feel better. Not from something outside, but a change inside.

The following page has your 10-day Jumpstart Plan. After that are descriptions of the body movements or activities not already covered with Habits 1, 2, or 3.

DAY	HABIT 1: BODY	HABIT 2: MIND	HABIT 3: SPIRIT
1	NECK	10 soft breaths 1 x day	Research affirmations. Select 3 and post in 3 areas, such as bedroom, kitchen, or bathroom).
2	TOE TOUCH	10 soft breaths 1x day	Read affirmations hourly.

3	NECK & TRUNK	10 soft breaths 2x day	Read 1 affirmation hourly. Research meditations.
4	WAIST	10 soft breaths 2x day	Try a 10-minute meditation.
5	TRUNK & WAIST	20 soft breaths 1x day	Use an affirmation to try a 1-minute mediation three or four times during the day.
6	LEGS	10 soft breaths 2x day	Try a 15-minute meditation.
7	TOE TOUCH	10 soft breaths 2x day	Use an affirmation to try a 1-minute mediation three or four times during the day.
8	NOSE & LEGS	10 soft breaths 3x day	Try a 10-minute meditation.
9	TRUNK & WAIST	10 soft breaths 3x day	Try 2 10-minute meditations (am/pm).
10	TOTAL BODY	10 soft breaths 3x day	Try a 20-minute meditation.

TOTAL BODY RESET

This is a 10-minute session that includes a 4-movement whole-body reset. For extra credit, you can start with a 10 count Breath and end with a focus on gratitude or counting acts of kindness.

You can do this lying down. This can be a great routine to end your day or as a midday reset. Please modify any movement or component to best meet your needs.

Movement #1   Muscle Target: Neck

- Starting position: Lie on the floor or bed face up. Spread your feet a little wider than your hip joints. Rest your hands alongside your body. Keep your lower body as still as possible.
- Movement: Using only your nose, spell your name.
- Spell your name backward.
- Spell the words: I Am Still.
- Allow the body to rest completely in-between cycles.

Movement #2   Muscle Target: Trunk

- Starting position: Lie on your back with your knees bent and feet near the buttocks. Keep your lower body as still as possible as you rotate.
- Movement: Keeping your knees together allow the legs to slowly lower to the right as far as they will naturally fall.

When you feel a stretch begin, stop, and slowly lift them back to vertical.

- Cross the left leg fully over the right leg. Allow the legs to slowly lower to the right as far as they will naturally fall. When you feel a stretch begin, stop, and slowly lift them back to vertical.
- Leave the left leg entirely over the right leg. Roll your head to the left and extend your left arm upward above your head. Your nose should be close to your armpit.
- Your right arm is resting along your side. Allow the legs to lower, make it feel as pleasant as possible.
- Rest and slowly bring your legs, arm, and head back to the starting position. Allow the body to rest completely.
- Repeat for the left side. You can extend this movement by tipping your hip forward.

Movement #3. Muscle Target: Waist

- Starting position: Lie on your back face up. Spread your feet a little wider than your hip joints. Reach both arms straight above your head against the floor, spreading them wider than your shoulders. Your body will look like a giant X.
- Movement: Slowly lengthen your right leg, sliding the heel down the floor.
- Relaxing the right leg, slowly lengthen your left arm above the head, sliding it along the floor.
- Repeat for the left leg, right hand.

- Complete the movement by putting the four activities together in a rounded fashion. Stretch the left arm upward, then rest. Stretch the left leg downward, then rest. Stretch the right arm upward, then rest. Stretch the left arm upward, then rest. Complete the 4-point cycle 3 times.
- Allow the body to rest completely in-between cycles.

Movement #4   Muscle Target: Full Body Integration

- Starting Position: Lying on your back, legs lowered, fingers interlaced behind the head.
- Raise the right leg. Slowly return to the floor.
- Repeat for the left leg.
- Repeat. Raise the right leg. This time bring your chin to your chest. Flatten the back and lift the head forward while raising the right leg. Slowly return to the floor Repeat for the left leg.
- Allow the body to rest completely.

That's the end of this guide. Thanks for reading. I hope you have some easy, enjoyable new tools to help you rest. It is more important than ever to reclaim this sacred part of yourself. I hope you will share your experiences with me.

Until then,

To all of you, I offer quietness.

To all of you, I offer gentleness.

To all of you, I offer peace of mind.